GW00707890

Gentle
Thoughts

Compiled by
Beth Mende Conny

PETER PAUPER PRESS, INC.
WHITE PLAINS, NEW YORK

Copyright © 1993
Peter Pauper Press, Inc.
202 Mamaroneck Avenue
White Plains, NY 10601
All rights reserved
ISBN 0-88088-760-5
Printed in China
14   13   12   11   10   9   8

GENTLE
THOUGHTS

Angels fly because they take themselves lightly.

Anonymous

Hospitality consists in a little fire, a little food, and an immense quiet.
Ralph Waldo Emerson

*Talk happiness. The world
is sad enough
Without your woe. No path
is wholly rough.*
　　　Ella Wheeler Wilcox

Darkness is merely the absence of light, and fear is merely the absence of love.
Marianne Williamson

Sometimes it proves the highest understanding not to understand.

Baltasar Gracián

Every education is a kind of inward journey.

Albert Gore, Jr.

I avoid looking forward or backward, and try to keep looking upward.
Charlotte Brontë

Until we lose ourselves there is no hope of finding ourselves.

Henry Miller

Man and woman may only enter Paradise hand in hand. Together, the myth tells us, they left it and together must they return.

Richard Garnett

Knowledge of what is possible is the beginning of happiness.

George Santayana

You have to leave room in life to dream.

Buffy Sainte-Marie

*Grief can take care of itself,
but to get the full value of a
joy you must have some-
body to divide it with.*

Mark Twain

We are all born for love. It is the principle of existence, and its only end.

Benjamin Disraeli

What sunshine is to flowers, smiles are to humanity. They are but trifles, to be sure, but, scattered along life's pathway, the good they do is inconceivable.

Joseph Addison

The best creed we can have is charity toward the creeds of others.

Josh Billings

When you cease to make a contribution you begin to die.

Eleanor Roosevelt

*The delights of self-discovery
are always available.*

Gail Sheehy

It's important that people know what you stand for. It's equally important that they know what you won't stand for.

Mary Waldrop

Speak only well of people
and you need never whisper.
　　　　　Fortune Cookie

Little said is soonest mended.
George Wither

Love is a fruit in season at all times.

Mother Teresa

A happy life is one spent in learning, earning and yearning.

Lillian Gish

When we face our fears and let ourselves know our connection to the power that is in us and beyond us, we learn courage.
Anne Wilson Schaef

It is much more productive to spend time searching for purpose and meaning than searching for happiness.

Dr. Gerald Kushel

Nothing is interesting if you are not interested.

Helen MacInnes

*Acceptance does not preclude
change, it precludes
remaining in conflict.*
Hugh and Gayle Prather

Perfection is attained by slow degrees; she requires the hand of time.

Voltaire

A handful of pine-seed will cover mountains with the green majesty of forest. I too will set my face to the wind and throw my handful of seed on high.

William Sharp

There is nothing stronger in the world than gentleness.

Han Suyin

When we are flat on our backs there is no way to look but up.

Roger W. Babson

*Joy is the holy fire that
keeps our purpose warm
and our intelligence aglow.*
Helen Keller

*There is no meaning to life
except the meaning man
gives his life by the
unfolding of his powers.*
Erich Fromm

A diamond is a lump of coal that stuck with it.

Anonymous

*The best portion of a good
    man's life,—
His little nameless,
    unremembered acts
Of kindness and of love.*
        William Wordsworth

To see the world in a grain of sand,
And a heaven in a wild flower;
Hold infinity in the palm of your hand,
And eternity in an hour.

William Blake

*Troubles are often the tools
by which God fashions us
for better things.*
Henry Ward Beecher

In the depths of winter, I finally learned that within me there lay an invincible summer.

Albert Camus

Friendship means no separate heart.
Hugh and Gayle Prather

*Kindness is the oil that takes
the friction out of life.*

Anonymous

*Only when one is connected
to one's own core is one
connected to others, I am
beginning to discover. And,
for me, the core, the inner
spring, can best be refound
through solitude.*
Anne Morrow Lindbergh

Failures are like skinned knees—painful but superficial.

Ross Perot

Without faith a man can do nothing; with it all things are possible.

Sir William Osler

The good neighbor looks beyond the external accidents and discerns those inner qualities that make all men human and, therefore, brothers.

Martin Luther King, Jr.

Three things in human life are important. The first is to be kind. The second is to be kind. And the third is to be kind.

Henry James

The quieter you become the more you can hear.

Baba Ram Dass

If I had but two loaves of bread, I would sell one and buy hyacinths, for they would feed my soul.

The Koran

We know nothing of to-morrow; our business is to be good and happy today.
Samuel Taylor Coleridge

You must forgive those who transgress against you before you can look to forgiveness from Above.

The Talmud

Go not abroad for happiness.
   For see,
It is a flower that
   blossoms at thy door.

   Minot J. Savage

*If I had my life to live over,
I would start barefoot earlier
in the spring and stay that
way later in the fall. I would
go to more dances. I would
ride more merry-go-rounds.
I would pick more daisies.*

Nadine Stair

With mirth and laughter let old wrinkles come.
William Shakespeare

*Change is an easy panacea.
It takes character to stay in
one place and be happy
there.*

Elizabeth Clarke Dunn

*The most beautiful thing we
can experience is the mystery.*
Albert Einstein

Real generosity toward the future consists in giving all to what is present.

Albert Camus

*Forgiveness is the key to
action and freedom.*

Hannah Arendt

Keep your face always toward the sunshine, and the shadows will fall behind you.

Anonymous

To love is the great amulet that makes this world a garden.
Robert Louis Stevenson

It is not death that a man should fear, but he should fear never beginning to live.
Marcus Aurelius

One must look for one thing only, to find many.

Cesare Pavese

It is only with the heart that one can see rightly; what is essential is invisible to the eye.
Antoine de Saint-Exupéry

Patience is the key to joy.
Fortune Cookie

The tree which needs two arms to span its girth sprang from the tiniest shoot. Yon tower, nine stories high, rose from a little mound of earth. A journey of a thousand miles began with a single step.

Lao-tse

*The creation of a thousand
forests is in one acorn.*
Ralph Waldo Emerson

*You can't change the music
of your soul.*
    Katharine Hepburn

Most persons would succeed in small things if they were not troubled with great ambitions.

Henry Wadsworth Longfellow

*The great thing about
getting older is that you
don't lose all the other ages
you've been.*
Madeleine L'Engle

You will find, as you look back upon your life, that the moments that stand out, the moments when you have really lived, are the moments when you have done things in the spirit of Love.

Henry Drummond